Let's Go to the BANK

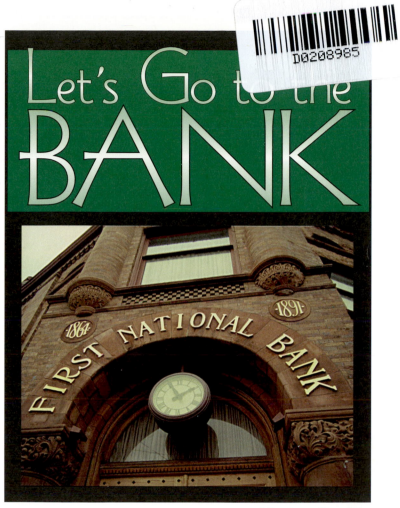

Kathy Smith

The Rosen Publishing Group, Inc.
New York

A bank is a place where you can keep your money. A bank can also **lend** people money.

Long ago, some people did not use money. They traded things they had, like eggs and milk, for things they needed, like cloth and buttons.

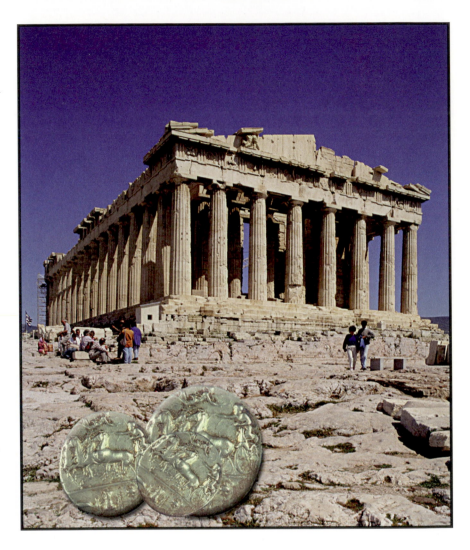

As far back as 2,500 years ago, some people began to trade with coins. Coins were easy to carry. They were kept in **temples**, which became the first banks.

Today, most towns and cities
have banks. Almost everyone
uses a bank in some way.

When you keep your money in a bank, it might be stored in a big **safe**. Only the people who work at the bank can go into the safe.

The people who work at a bank
can help you keep a **record** of
your money. This record tells you
how much money you have in
the bank.

Some of the people working
at the bank are called **tellers**.
Tellers help people put money
in and take money out of the
bank.

Many people borrow money from the bank. This money is called a **loan**.

When people get a loan from a bank, they promise to pay money back to the bank a little at a time. People use loans to buy large things, like cars.

You can use a bank too. You can keep your own money in a bank. Ask your mom or dad how!

GLOSSARY

lend   To let someone use something for a while, until they give it back.

loan   The money a bank gives a person that the person pays back a little at a time.

record   Something written down so you can easily remember it.

safe   A big room in a bank where money is stored.

teller   A bank worker who takes in, gives out, and counts money.

temple   A building where people go to pray.